TO: phyL - O

FROM: AUT
gloria
◁

KEEP
CALM
AND
CARRY
ON

BY EVELYN BEILENSON

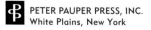

PETER PAUPER PRESS, INC.
White Plains, New York

Designed by David Cole Wheeler

Copyright © 2013
Peter Pauper Press, Inc.
202 Mamaroneck Avenue
White Plains, NY 10601
All rights reserved
ISBN 978-1-4413-1253-2
Printed in China

7

Visit us at www.peterpauper.com

INTRODUCTION

The sky is falling! The sky is falling!

—CHICKEN LITTLE

We live in challenging times. Worries and stresses are tough enough, but we only make them worse when we take them to heart. Some fears are real, some imagined, but no fear is too big to laugh at, or at least to smack upside the head. As Jon Kabat-Zinn has written, "You can't stop the waves, but you can learn to surf."

KEEP
CALM
AND
CARRY
ON

Inspired by the British World War II poster, *Keep Calm and Carry On*, which was meant to provide a sense of calm during uncertain times, this little volume exhorts us to "Buck up, chap!" despite the obstacles life slings our way. Here are words of comfort and humor from a pantheon of original thinkers, from Buddha to Yoda and from Winston Churchill to Al Franken.

KEEP CALM? RIGHT ON!

It's easier to put on slippers than to carpet the whole world.

AL FRANKEN

It just wouldn't be a picnic without the ants.

AUTHOR UNKNOWN

Fill your life with worries and there's little room for dreams.

BETH MENDE CONNY

Life is 10 percent what happens to you and 90 percent how you react to it.

CHARLES R. SWINDOLL

When we are no longer able to change a situation, we are challenged to change ourselves.

VIKTOR FRANKL

Life does not have to be easy to be wonderful.

AUTHOR UNKNOWN

Try not.
Do or do not.
There is no try.

YODA

At the height of laughter, the universe is flung into a kaleidoscope of new possibilities.

JEAN HOUSTON

The most effective way to cope with change is to help create it.

L. W. LYNETT

When it is dark enough, you can see the stars.

CHARLES A. BEARD

Music has charms to soothe a savage breast, to soften rocks, or bend a knotted oak.

WILLIAM CONGREVE

The crisis of today is the joke of tomorrow.

H. G. WELLS

Inward calm cannot
be maintained unless
physical strength
is constantly and
intelligently
replenished.

BUDDHA

Leave your worries behind. Go on a vacation—with yourself.

BETH MENDE CONNY

A diamond is a chunk of coal that is made good under pressure.

HENRY KISSINGER

Since the house is on fire, let us warm ourselves.

ITALIAN PROVERB

I've missed more than 9,000 shots in my career. I've lost almost 300 games. Twenty-six times I've been trusted to take the game-winning shot and missed. I've failed over and over and over again in my life. And that is why I succeed.

MICHAEL JORDAN

People are resilient.
After all, every person
born has recovered
from nine months on
life support.

ROBERT BRAULT

Never waste a good crisis.

HILLARY CLINTON

When down in
the mouth,
remember Jonah.
He came out
all right.

THOMAS EDISON

Humor can help you cope with the unbearable so that you can stay on the bright side of things until the bright side actually comes along.

ALLEN KLEIN

Affirm divine calmness and peace, and send out only thoughts of love and goodwill if you want to live in peace and harmony. Never get angry, for anger poisons your system.

PARAMAHANSA YOGANANDA

When it gets too much, I just walk the beaches of Sydney and get calm again. You just grab your surfboard, splash in those waves and feel happy to be alive. That's what really matters.

TONI COLLETTE

Nobody ever cleared a path for themselves by giving up.

ALICIA BESSETTE

When written in Chinese, the word "crisis" is composed of two characters— one represents danger and one represents opportunity.

JOHN F. KENNEDY

You can turn
painful situations
around through
laughter. If you
can find humor
in anything, even
poverty, you can
survive it.

BILL COSBY

When angry, count four; when very angry, swear.

MARK TWAIN

People get so in the habit of worry that if you save them from drowning and put them on a bank to dry in the sun with hot chocolate and muffins they wonder whether they are catching cold.

JOHN JAY CHAPMAN

When everything
seems to be going
against you, remember
that the airplane
takes off against the
wind, not with it.

HENRY FORD

Life is not a matter of having good cards, but of playing a poor hand well.

ROBERT LOUIS STEVENSON

The cyclone derives its powers from a calm center. So does a person.

NORMAN VINCENT PEALE

Forget your mistakes, but remember what they taught you.

DOROTHY GALYEAN

Many an obstacle is really a stepping stone.

BETH MENDE CONNY

Inside of a ring
or out, ain't nothing
wrong with going
down. It's staying
down that's wrong.

MUHAMMAD ALI

Even in the middle of
a hurricane, the bottom
of the sea is calm.
As the storm rages and
the winds howl, the deep
waters sway in gentle
rhythm, a light movement
of fish and plant life.
Below there is no storm.

WAYNE MULLER

My advice to you is not to inquire why or whither, but just enjoy your ice cream while it's on your plate— that's my philosophy.

THORNTON WILDER

Stress is an ignorant state. It believes that everything is an emergency. Nothing is that important.

NATALIE GOLDBERG

Laughter is the sun
that drives winter from
the human face.

VICTOR HUGO

I don't feel any pressure. I just try to stay calm, follow my game plan, and try not to overthrow.

DWIGHT GOODEN

Nothing is permanent in this wicked world—not even our troubles.

CHARLIE CHAPLIN

Anything that gets you to release the stress in your life and really laugh is worthwhile.

LUCIE ARNAZ

A truly happy person is one who can enjoy the scenery on a detour.

EVELYN LOEB

My life has been full of terrible misfortunes, most of which never happened.

MICHEL DE MONTAIGNE

You can avoid having ulcers by adapting to the situation: If you fall in the mud puddle, check your pockets for fish.

AUTHOR UNKNOWN

Take up gardening—clear, prune, and weed worries from your life.

BETH MENDE CONNY

If you're in a bad situation, don't worry it'll change.
If you're in a good situation, don't worry it'll change.

JOHN A. SIMONE, SR.

Sometimes I think my life would make a great TV movie. It even has the part where they say, "Stand by. We are experiencing temporary difficulties."

ROBERT BRAULT

Pressure and stress is the common cold of the psyche.

ANDREW DENTON

The more tranquil a man becomes, the greater is his success, his influence, his power for good. Calmness of mind is one of the beautiful jewels of wisdom.

JAMES ALLEN

If you're going through hell, keep going.

WINSTON CHURCHILL

Life is like a blanket too short. You pull it up and your toes rebel, you yank it down and shivers meander about your shoulder; but cheerful folks manage to draw their knees up and pass a very comfortable night.

MARION HOWARD

I quit being afraid when my first venture failed and the sky didn't fall down.

ALLEN H. NEUHARTH

Worry never robs tomorrow of its sorrow, it only saps today of its joy.

LEO BUSCAGLIA

The truth is that our finest moments are most likely to occur when we are feeling deeply uncomfortable, unhappy, or unfulfilled. For it is only in such moments, propelled by our discomfort, that we are likely to step out of our ruts and start searching for different ways or truer answers.

M. SCOTT PECK

**Calm self-confidence
is as far from conceit
as the desire to earn a
decent living is remote
from greed.**

CHANNING POLLOCK

What if we just acted like everything was easy?

MARY ANNE RADMACHER

Twenty years from now you will be more disappointed by the things that you didn't do than by the ones you did do. So throw off the bowlines. Sail away from the safe harbor. Catch the trade winds in your sails. Explore. Dream. Discover.

H. JACKSON BROWN, JR.

Let go of what's beyond your control and it will no longer control you.

BETH MENDE CONNY

Never be in a hurry;
do everything quietly
and in a calm spirit.
Do not lose your
inner peace for
anything whatsoever,
even if your whole world
seems upset.

SAINT FRANCIS DE SALES

The only thing we have to fear is fear itself.

FRANKLIN D. ROOSEVELT

Life is not about waiting for the storms to pass ... it's about learning to dance in the rain.

VIVIAN GREENE

You should treat all disasters as if they were trivialities but never treat a triviality as if it were a disaster.

QUENTIN CRISP

What I dream of is an art of balance, or purity and serenity . . . a soothing, calming influence on the mind, rather like a good armchair which provides relaxation from physical fatigue.

HENRI MATISSE

If you don't like something, change it; if you can't change it, change the way you think about it.

MARY ENGELBREIT

Hard times don't create heroes. It is during the hard times when the "hero" within us is revealed.

BOB RILEY

Life is a tragedy when seen in close-up, but a comedy in long-shot.

CHARLIE CHAPLIN

When we can begin to take our failures non-seriously, it means we are ceasing to be afraid of them. It is of immense importance to learn to laugh at ourselves.

KATHERINE MANSFIELD

Worry,
like junk food,
adds unneeded
weight.

BETH MENDE CONNY

My father used to say to me, "Whenever you get into a jam, whenever you get into a crisis or an emergency, become the calmest person in the room and you'll be able to figure your way out of it."

RUDOLPH GIULIANI

The darkest hour has only sixty minutes.

MORRIS MANDEL

Life's not always fair.
Sometimes you get a
splinter even sliding
down a rainbow.

TERRI GUILLEMETS

Music is moonlight in the gloomy night of life.

JEAN PAUL RICHTER

Don't underestimate the value of Doing Nothing, of just going along, listening to all the things you can't hear, and not bothering.

PIGLET FROM A. A. MILNE'S
WINNIE-THE-POOH

Your success and happiness lie in you. Resolve to keep happy, and your joy and you shall form an invincible host against difficulties.

HELEN KELLER

Always behave like a duck—keep calm and unruffled on the surface but paddle like the devil underneath.

JACOB BRAUDE